There's an afghan for everyone in the family from Baby to Dad. Choose from a variety of designs, including lacy, textured afghans and those with geometric designs.

LEISURE ARTS, INC. • Maumelle, Arkansas

Diamonds Baby Blanket

EASY +

Finished Measurement: 40½" x 42½" (103 cm x 108 cm)

SHOPPING LIST

Yarn (Light Weight) 3

[5 ounces, 362 yards
(140 grams, 331 meters) per skein**]**:

- ☐ Main Color (Grey) - 3 skeins

[4.2 ounces, 310 yards
(120 grams, 284 meters) per skein**]**:

- ☐ Color A (Variegated Purple) - 1 skein
- ☐ Color B (Variegated Blue) - 1 skein

Crochet Hook

- ☐ Size H (5 mm) **or** size needed for gauge

GAUGE INFORMATION

Gauge Swatch: 2" (5 cm) diagonally
Work same as Block #1.

The blanket is made up of afghan stitch blocks, beginning at the center. Use diagram as a guide.

MAIN COLOR CENTER

BLOCK #1

With Main Color, ch 6.

Row 1 (Right side)**:** Working in back ridge of chs *(Fig. 1, page 30)*, insert hook in second ch from hook *(Fig. A)*, YO and pull up a loop, continue to pull up a loop in each ch across keeping all loops on hook *(Fig. B)*: 6 loops.

To Close: YO and draw through one loop on hook, ★ YO and draw through 2 loops on hook *(Fig. C)*; repeat from ★ across until one loop remains on hook.

Fig. A

Fig. B

Fig. C

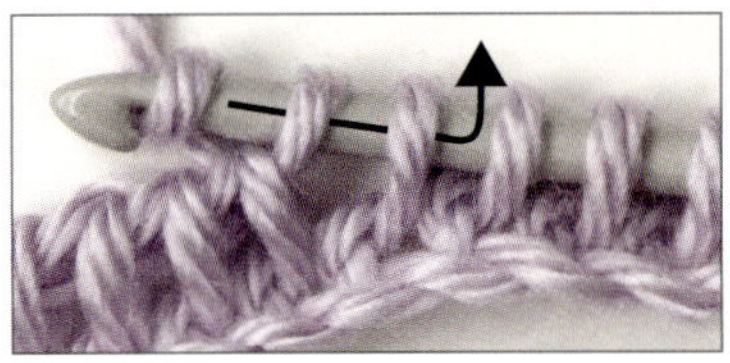

Note: Loop a short piece of yarn around any stitch to mark Row 1 as **right** side. All rows are worked with right side facing.

Diagram

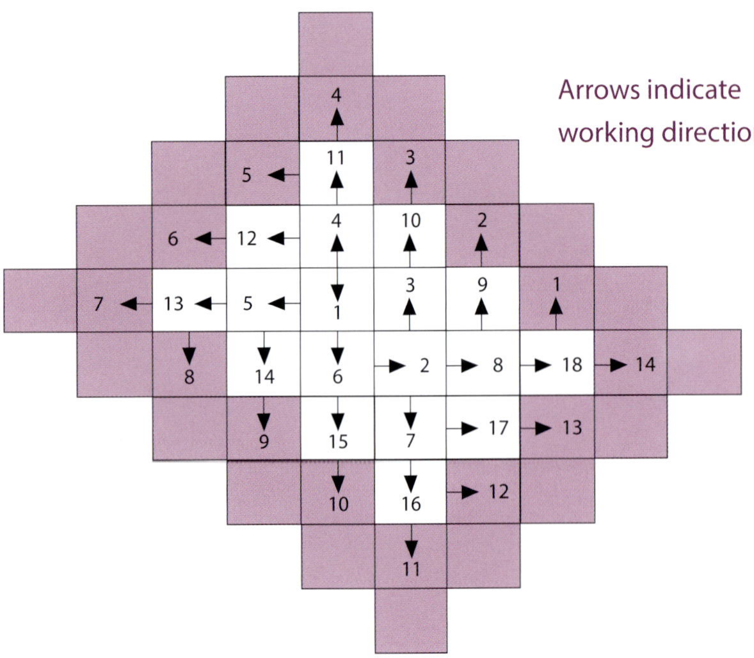

Arrows indicate working direction.

Rows 2-4: Skip first vertical bar, insert hook from **right** to **left** under next vertical bar, *(Fig. D)*, YO and pull up a loop, continue to pull up a loop in each vertical bar across: 6 loops.

To Close: Work same as Row 1.

Fig. D

Row 5: Ch 1, skip first vertical bar, ★ pull up a loop in next vertical bar and draw through loop on hook (**slip st made**); repeat from ★ across.

Do **not** finish off at end of Blocks unless instructed.

BLOCK #2

Ch 6.

Row 1: Pull up a loop in back ridge of second ch from hook and in each ch across (6 loops on hook); close.

Rows 2-4: Skip first vertical bar, pull up a loop in next 5 vertical bars (6 loops on hook); close.

Row 5: Ch 1, skip first vertical bar, slip st in next 5 vertical bars.

BLOCK #3

Row 1: Ch 1, skip first row, working **behind** vertical bars at edge, pull up a loop in next 4 rows and in beginning ch (6 loops on hook); to close, pull up a loop in row **behind** vertical bar at edge of Block #1 **and** draw loop through one loop on hook, (YO and draw through 2 loops on hook) across.

Rows 2-4: Skip first vertical bar, pull up a loop in next 5 vertical bars (6 loops on hook); close same as Row 1.

Row 5: Ch 1, skip first vertical bar, slip st in next 4 vertical bars, insert hook under last vertical bar **and** in last row on Block #1, YO and draw through all 3 loops.

BLOCK #4

Row 1: Pull up a loop in Back Loop Only of next 5 sts on next Block ***(Fig. 2, page 30)*** (6 loops on hook); close.

Rows 2-4: Skip first vertical bar, pull up a loop in next 5 vertical bars (6 loops on hook); close.

Row 5: Ch 1, skip first vertical bar, slip st in next 5 vertical bars.

BLOCK #5

Row 1: Ch 1, skip first row, slip st in vertical bar at end of next 4 rows and in sp between Blocks, pull up a loop in Back Loop Only of next 5 sts on next Block (6 loops on hook); close.

Rows 2-4: Skip first vertical bar, pull up a loop in next 5 vertical bars (6 loops on hook); close.

Row 5: Ch 1, skip first vertical bar, slip st in next 5 vertical bars.

BLOCK #6

Row 1: Ch 1, skip first row, slip st in vertical bar at end of next 4 rows and in sp between Blocks, pull up a loop in Back Loop Only of next 5 sts on next Block (6 loops on hook); to close, pull up a loop in Back Loop Only of first st on next Block and draw loop through one loop on hook, (YO and draw through 2 loops on hook) across.

Rows 2-4: Skip first vertical bar, pull up a loop in next 5 vertical bars (6 loops on hook); close same as Row 1.

Row 5: Ch 1, skip first vertical bar, slip st in next 4 vertical bars, insert hook under last vertical bar **and** in Back Loop Only of last st on Block, YO and draw through both sts and loop on hook.

BLOCK #7

Work same as Block #4.

BLOCK #8

Row 1: Ch 1, skip first row, slip st in vertical bar at end of next 4 rows and in sp between Blocks, pull up a loop in Back Loop Only of next 5 sts on next Block (6 loops on hook); close.

Rows 2-4: Skip first vertical bar, pull up a loop in next 5 vertical bars (6 loops on hook); close.

Row 5: Ch 1, skip first vertical bar, slip st in next 5 vertical bars.

Ten Blocks are worked around the first 8 Blocks to form the center.

BLOCK #9

Row 1: Ch 1, skip first row, working **behind** vertical bars at edge, pull up a loop in next 4 rows and in sp between Blocks (6 loops on hook); to close, pull up a loop in Back Loop Only of first st on next Block and draw through one loop on hook, (YO and draw through 2 loops on hook) across.

Rows 2-4: Skip first vertical bar, pull up a loop in next 5 vertical bars (6 loops on hook); close same as Row 1.

Row 5: Ch 1, skip first vertical bar, slip st in next 4 vertical bars, insert hook under last vertical bar **and** in Back Loop Only of last st on next Block, YO and draw through both sts and loop on hook.

BLOCK #10

Row 1: Pull up a loop in Back Loop Only of next 5 sts on next Block (6 loops on hook); to close, pull up a loop in Back Loop Only of next st at edge of next Block and draw loop through one loop on hook, (YO and draw through 2 loops on hook) across.

Rows 2-4: Skip first vertical bar, pull up a loop in next 5 vertical bars (6 loops on hook); close same as Row 1.

Row 5: Ch 1, skip first vertical bar, slip st in next 4 vertical bars, insert hook under last vertical bar **and** in Back Loop Only at edge of next Block, YO and draw loop through all 3 loops.

BLOCK #11 (Corner Block)

Row 1: Pull up a loop in Back Loop Only of next 5 sts on next Block (6 loops on hook); close.

Rows 2-4: Skip first vertical bar, pull up a loop in next 5 vertical bars (6 loops on hook); close.

Row 5: Ch 1, skip first vertical bar, slip st in next 5 vertical bars.

BLOCK #12

Row 1: Ch 1, skip first row, slip st in vertical bar at end of next 4 rows and in sp between Blocks, pull up a loop in Back Loop Only of next 5 sts on next Block (6 loops on hook); to close, pull up a loop in Back Loop Only of first st on next Block and draw loop through one loop on hook, (YO and draw through 2 loops on hook) across.

Rows 2-4: Skip first vertical bar, pull up a loop in next 5 vertical bars (6 loops on hook); close same as Row 1.

Row 5: Ch 1, skip first vertical bar, slip st in next 4 vertical bars, insert hook under last vertical bar **and** in Back Loop Only of last st on Block, YO and draw through both sts and loop on hook.

BLOCK #13 (Corner Block)

Work same as Block #11.

BLOCK #14

Work same as Block #12.

BLOCK #15

Work same as Block #10.

BLOCK #16 (Corner Block)

Work same as Block #11.

BLOCK #17

Work same as Block #12.

BLOCK #18 (Corner Block)

Work same as Block #11.

Finish off.

COLOR A SECTION

BLOCK #1

Row 1: With **right** side facing, using Color A, and working **behind** vertical bars at edge of last Block made, pull up a loop in all 5 rows and in sp between Blocks (6 loops on hook); to close, pull up a loop in Back Loop Only of first st on next Block and draw through one loop on hook, (YO and draw through 2 loops on hook) across.

Rows 2-5: Work same as Block #9 on Center.

BLOCKS #2 & 3

Work same as Block #10 of Center.

BLOCK #4 (Corner Block)

Work same as Block #11 of Center.

BLOCK #5

Work same as Block #12 of Center.

BLOCK #6

Work same as Block #10 of Center.

BLOCK #7 (Corner Block)

Work same as Block #11 of Center.

BLOCK #8

Work same as Block #12 of Center.

BLOCKS #9 & 10

Work same as Block #10 of Center.

BLOCK #11 (Corner Block)

Work same as Block #11 of Center.

BLOCK #12

Work same as Block #12 of Center.

BLOCK #13

Work same as Block #10 of Center.

BLOCK #14 (Corner Block)

Work same as Block #11 of Center.

First Round of Section is complete.

BLOCKS #15-32

Work second round of section in same manner as first.

Finish off.

REMAINING SECTIONS

Work in same manner as Color A Section working one more Block across each edge and working in the following color sequence: Main Color, Color B, Main Color, Color A, Main Color, Color B, Main Color.

Do **not** finish off after last Block.

EDGING

Rnd 1: Ch 1, sc in last st made, ★ † ch 2, (dc, ch 3, dc) in st between Blocks, ch 2, sc in corner st of next Block †, repeat from † to † across side, ch 5, skip next 3 sts, sc in next st; repeat from ★ 2 times **more**, then repeat from † to † across last side, ch 5, skip next 3 sts; join with slip st to first sc.

Rnd 2: Ch 1, sc in same st as joining, ch 2, ★ † skip next ch-2 sp, (dc, ch 3, dc) in next ch-3 sp, ch 2, skip next ch-2 sp, sc in next sc, ch 2 †, repeat from † to † across to next corner ch-5 sp, (dc, ch 3, dc) in corner ch-5 sp, ch 2, sc in next sc, ch 2; repeat from ★ 2 times **more**, then repeat from † to † across last side, (dc, ch 3, dc) in corner ch-5 sp, ch 2; join with slip st to first sc.

Rnd 3: Ch 1, 2 sc in next ch-2 sp, (2 sc, ch 3, slip st in third ch from hook, 2 sc) in next ch-3 sp, ★ 2 sc in each of next 2 ch-2 sps, (2 sc, ch 3, slip st in third ch from hook, 2 sc) in next ch-3 sp; repeat from ★ around to last ch-2 sp, 2 sc in last sp; join with slip st to first sc, finish off.

Design by Cheryl A. Riley.

Royal Mosaic

EASY

Finished Measurement: 48" x 63½" (122 cm x 161.5 cm)

SHOPPING LIST

Yarn (Medium Weight) 4

[3.5 ounces, 200 yards
(100 grams, 182 meters)
per skein**]**:

- ☐ Color A (Purple) - 8 skeins
- ☐ Color B (Teal) - 9 skeins

Crochet Hook

- ☐ Size I (5.5 mm)
  or size needed for gauge

GAUGE INFORMATION

In pattern,

13 sts and 16 rows = 4" (10 cm)

Gauge Swatch: 4" (10 cm) square

With Color A, ch 14.

Work same as Body for 16 rows: 13 sts.

Finish off.

STITCH GUIDE

LONG DOUBLE CROCHET
(abbreviated LDC)

YO, working **around** previous 2 rows ***(Fig. 5, page 31)***, insert hook in sc indicated in row **below**, YO and pull up a loop even with last sc made, (YO and draw through 2 loops on hook) twice ***(Fig. A)***.

Fig. A

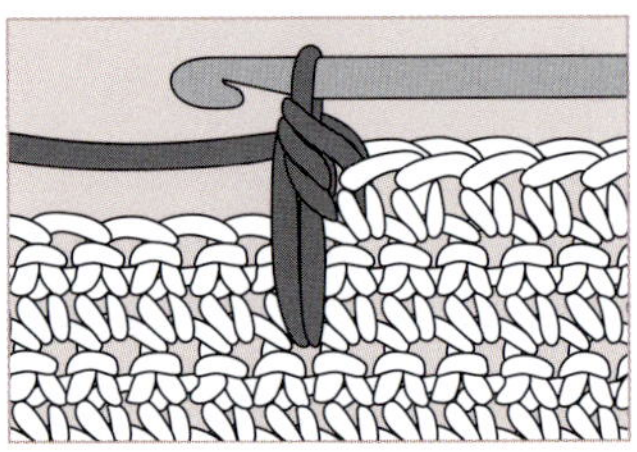

BODY

With Color A, ch 150.

Row 1: Sc in second ch from hook and in each ch across: 149 sc.

Row 2 (Right side)**:** Ch 1, turn; sc in each sc across.

Note: Loop a short piece of yarn around any stitch to mark Row 2 as **right** side.

Row 3: Ch 1, turn; sc in each sc across changing to Color B in last sc ***(Fig. 7a, page 31)***; do **not** cut Color A.

Carry unused color along edge.

Row 4: Ch 1, turn; sc in first sc, working **around** previous 2 rows ***(Fig. 5, page 31)***, work LDC in third sc on Row 1, skip next sc on previous row (behind LDC), sc in next sc, work LDC in same st as last LDC, skip next sc on previous row, sc in next sc, ★ working **around** previous 2 rows, work LDC in fourth sc from last LDC on Row 1, skip next sc on previous row, sc in next sc, work LDC in same st as last LDC, skip next sc on previous row, sc in next sc; repeat from ★ across: 37 LDC groups.

Row 5: Ch 1, turn; sc in each st across changing to Color A in last sc: 149 sc.

Row 6: Ch 1, turn; sc in first 4 sc, working **around** previous 2 rows, work LDC in Color A sc 2 rows **below** next sc, skip next sc on previous row, ★ sc in next 3 sc, working **around** previous 2 rows, work LDC in Color A sc 2 rows **below** next sc, skip next sc on previous row; repeat from ★ across to last 4 sc, sc in last 4 sc: 36 LDC and 113 sc.

Row 7: Ch 1, turn; sc in each st across changing to Color B in last sc: 149 sc.

Row 8: Ch 1, turn; sc in first sc, working **around** previous 2 rows, work LDC in third sc on last Color B row, skip next sc on previous row, sc in next sc, work LDC in same st as last LDC, skip next sc on previous row, sc in next sc, ★ working **around** previous 2 rows, work LDC in fourth sc from last LDC on last Color B row, skip next sc on previous row, sc in next sc, work LDC in same st as last LDC, skip next sc on previous row, sc in next sc; repeat from ★ across: 37 LDC groups.

Repeat Rows 5-8 for pattern until Body measures approximately 61½" (156 cm) from beginning ch, ending by working Row 6.

Last 2 Rows: Ch 1, turn; sc in each st across; at end of last row, change to Color B.

EDGING

Rnd 1: Ch 1, do **not** turn; sc evenly across end of rows; working in free loops of beginning ch ***(Fig. 3b, page 30)***, 3 sc in first ch, sc in each ch across to last ch, 3 sc in last ch; sc evenly across end of rows working around carried strands; working across last row, 3 sc in first sc, sc in each sc across to last sc, 3 sc in last sc; join with slip st to first sc.

Rnd 2: Ch 1, turn; hdc in each sc around, working 3 hdc in center sc of each corner 3-sc group; drop Color B, with Color A, join with slip st to first hdc ***(Fig. 7b, page 31)***.

Rnd 3: Ch 1, turn; sc in sp **between** each hdc around ***(Fig. 4, page 31)***, working 2 sc **before** and **after** center hdc of each corner 3-hdc group; drop Color A, with Color B, join with slip st to first sc.

Rnd 4: Ch 1, do **not** turn; sc in each sc around, working 3 sc **between** both 2-sc groups at each corner; join with slip st to first sc, finish off.

Design by Margret Willson.

Square Gems

EASY +

Finished Measurement: 48" x 63" (122 cm x 160 cm)

SHOPPING LIST

Yarn (Medium Weight) MEDIUM 4

[7 ounces, 364 yards (198 grams, 333 meters) per skein]:

- ☐ Tan - 3 skeins
- ☐ Black - 2 skeins
- ☐ Green - 1 skein
- ☐ Orchid - 1 skein
- ☐ Burgundy - 1 skein
- ☐ Maroon - 1 skein
- ☐ Brown - 1 skein
- ☐ Gold - 1 skein

Crochet Hook

- ☐ Size J (6 mm)
  or size needed for gauge

Additional Supplies

- ☐ Yarn needle

GAUGE INFORMATION

Gauge Swatch: 7" (17.75 cm) square
Work same as Square.

STITCH GUIDE

FRONT POST SINGLE CROCHET ***(abbreviated FPsc)***

Insert hook from **front** to **back** around post of dc indicated *(Fig. 6, page 31)*, YO and pull up a loop, YO and draw through both loops on hook. Skip st **behind** FPsc.

BACK POST SINGLE CROCHET ***(abbreviated BPsc)***

Insert hook from **back** to **front** around post of dc indicated *(Fig. 6, page 31)*, YO and pull up a loop, YO and draw through both loops on hook. Skip st in **front** of BPsc.

SQUARE

(Make 6 Squares in **each**: Green, Orchid, Burgundy, Maroon, Brown, and Gold)

Ch 4; join with slip st to form a ring.

Rnd 1 (Right side)**:** Ch 3 **(counts as first dc, now and throughout)**, 2 dc in ring, ch 2, (3 dc in ring, ch 2) 3 times; join with slip st to first dc: 12 dc and 4 corner ch-2 sps.

Note: Loop a short piece of yarn around any stitch to mark Rnd 1 as **right** side.

Rnd 2: Ch 3, dc in next 2 dc, (2 dc, ch 2, 2 dc) in next corner ch-2 sp, ★ dc in next 3 dc, (2 dc, ch 2, 2 dc) in next corner ch-2 sp; repeat from ★ 2 times **more**; join with slip st to first dc: 28 dc and 4 corner ch-2 sps.

Rnds 3-5: Ch 3, ★ dc in next dc and in each dc across to next corner ch-2 sp, (2 dc, ch 2, 2 dc) in corner ch-2 sp; repeat from ★ 3 times **more**, dc in next dc and in each dc across; join with slip st to first dc: 76 dc and 4 corner ch-2 sps.

Finish off.

JOINING SQUARES

Using Placement Diagram as a guide, join Squares into 6 strips of 6 Squares each as follows:

Holding 2 Squares with **wrong** sides together, join Black with sc in first corner ch-2 sp on **front Square** ***(see Joining With Sc, page 30)***; ch 1, sc in corner ch-2 sp on **back Square**, ch 1, work FPsc around next dc on **front Square**, ch 1, ★ skip next dc on **back Square**, work BPsc around next dc, ch 1, skip next dc on **front Square**, work FPsc around next dc, ch 1; repeat from ★ across to last dc on **back Square**, skip last dc, sc in next corner ch-2 sp, ch 1, sc in next corner ch-2 sp on **front Square**; finish off.

BORDER

Work Border on top edge of five strips, leaving top strip without Border.

Row 1: With **right** side facing, join Tan with dc in first corner ch-2 sp on long edge ***(see Joining With Dc, page 30)***; dc in each dc across first Square, dc in next ch-2 sp, ★ dc in joining and in next ch-2 sp, dc in each dc across next Square, dc in next ch-2 sp; repeat from ★ across: 131 dc.

Rows 2-4: Ch 3, turn; dc in next dc and in each dc across.

Finish off.

PLACEMENT DIAGRAM

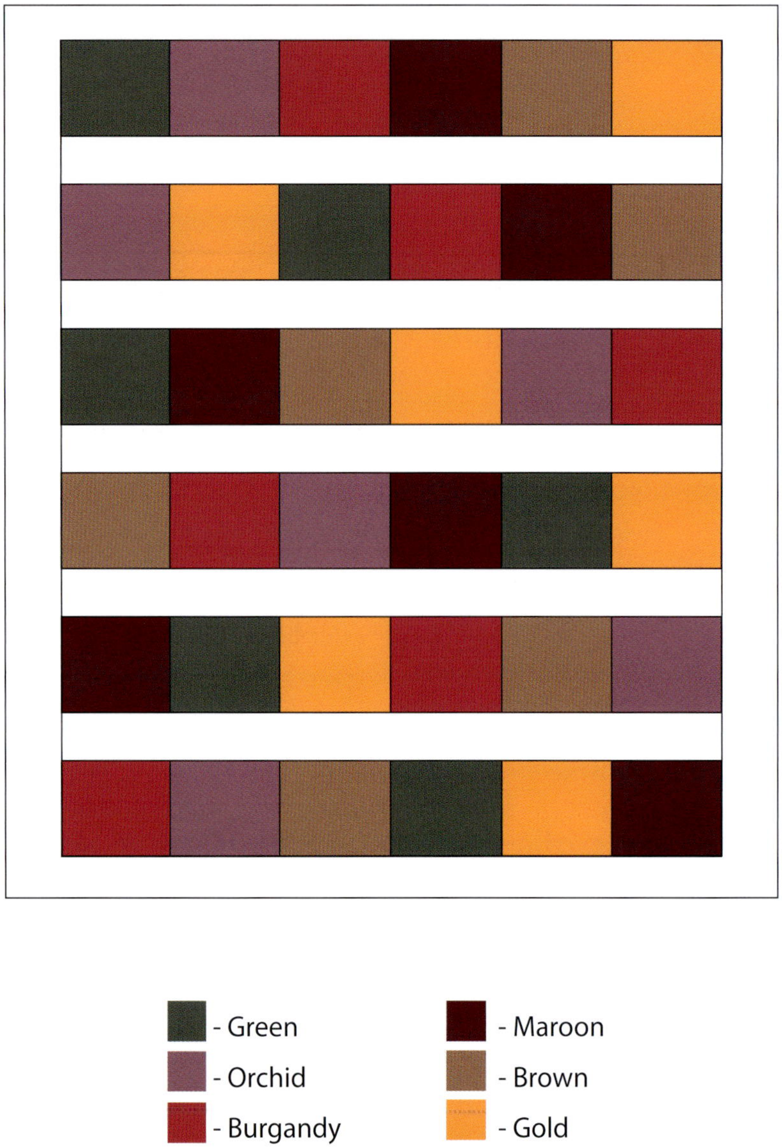

TRIM

JOINING STRIPS

Using Placement Diagram as a guide, join strips as Trim is worked as follows:

With **wrong** sides together, hold Border edge of one strip in **front** of the edge of Squares on the next strip.

Join Black with sc in first corner ch-2 sp on **back strip**; ch 1, work FPsc around first dc on Border of **front strip**, ch 1, work BPsc around next dc on **back strip**, ch 1, skip next dc on **front strip**, work FPsc around next dc, ch 1, ★ † skip next dc on **back strip**, work BPsc around next dc, ch 1, skip next dc on **front strip**, work FPsc around next dc, ch 1 †; repeat from † to † across to next joining on **back strip**, sc in joining, ch 1, skip next dc on **front strip**, work FPsc around next dc, ch 1, work BPsc around next dc on **back strip**, ch 1, skip next dc on **front strip**, work FPsc around next dc, ch 1; repeat from ★ 4 times **more**, then repeat from † to † across, sc in last ch-2 sp on **back strip**; finish off.

Join remaining Strips in same manner.

EDGING

Rnd 1: With **right** side facing and working across top edge, join Tan with dc in first dc; ★ dc in each dc across Square, † dc in next ch-2 sp, dc in joining and in next ch-2 sp, dc in each dc across Square †; repeat from † to † across to next corner ch-2 sp, 3 dc in ch-2 sp, skip next dc, dc in next dc and in each dc across Square, ♥ dc in next ch-2 sp and in Trim, work 6 dc evenly spaced across Border, dc in next Trim and in ch-2 sp, dc in each dc across Square ♥; repeat from ♥ to ♥ across to next corner ch-2 sp, 3 dc in ch-2 sp; repeat from ★ once **more**; join with slip st to first dc: 596 dc.

Rnds 2-4: Ch 3, turn; dc in each dc around working 3 dc in center dc of each corner 3-dc group; join with slip st to first dc: 620 dc.

Finish off.

Rnd 5: With **right** side facing, join Black with hdc in center dc of any corner 3-dc group *(see Joining With Hdc, page 30)*; hdc in same st, hdc in next dc and in each dc around, working 3 hdc in center dc of each corner 3-dc group, hdc in same st as first hdc; join with slip st to first hdc, do **not** finish off: 628 hdc.

OUTER EDGING TRIM

Ch 1, do **not** turn; work FPsc around same hdc as joining, ch 1, skip next hdc, work FPsc around dc in rnd **below** next hdc, ch 1, ★ † work FPsc around hdc in rnd **above** next dc, ch 1, work FPsc around dc in rnd **below** next hdc, ch 1 †; repeat from † to † across to corner dc on Rnd 4, work FPsc around corner hdc on Rnd 5, ch 1, skip next hdc, work FPsc around dc in rnd **below** next hdc, ch 1; repeat from ★ 2 times **more**, then repeat from † to † across; join with slip st to first FPsc, finish off.

INNER EDGING TRIM

With **right** side facing, join Black with sc around center dc of any corner 3-dc group on Rnd 1 of Edging; ★ ch 1, skip next dc on Square, work FPsc around next dc, ch 1, skip next dc on Rnd 1, work FPsc around next dc; repeat from ★ around, working around center dc of each corner ch-3 group; join with slip st to first sc, finish off.

Geometric Diamonds

INTERMEDIATE

Finished Measurement: 41½" x 56½" (105.5 cm x 143.5 cm)

SHOPPING LIST

Yarn (Medium Weight) 4

[3.5 ounces, 175 yards
(100 grams, 160 meters) per skein]:

- ☐ Color A (Grey) - 7 skeins

[3.5 ounces, 190 yards
(100 grams, 173 meters) per skein]:

- ☐ Color B (Blue) - 8 skeins

Crochet Hook

- ☐ Size J (6 mm)
  or size needed for gauge

GAUGE INFORMATION

In pattern,
13 sts and 16 rows = 4" (10 cm),

Gauge Swatch: 4" (10 cm) square
With Color A, ch 14.

Row 1 (Right side)**:** Sc in second ch from hook and in each ch across: 13 sc.

Row 2: Ch 1, turn; sc in each sc across changing to Color B in last sc *(Fig. 7a, page 31)*.

Row 3: Ch 1, turn; sc in BLO of each sc across *(Fig. 2, page 30)*.

Row 4: Ch 1, turn; sc in both loops of each sc across changing colors in last sc.

Rows 5-16: Repeat Rows 3 and 4, 6 times.

Finish off.

STITCH GUIDE

LONG DOUBLE CROCHET
(abbreviated LDC)

YO, working in **front** of previous 2 rows *(Fig. 5, page 31)*, insert hook in free loop of sc in row **below** *(Fig. 3a, page 30)*, YO and pull up a loop even with last sc made, (YO and draw through 2 loops on hook) twice. Skip sc behind LDC.

FOLLOWING A CHART

It is easier to follow a chart than written instructions and you can also see what the pattern looks like. The chart shows each stitch as a square. Visualize the chart as your fabric, beginning at the bottom edge. The pattern repeat is indicated by a heavy vertical line and letters. This section is to be repeated as specified.

For ease in following the chart, place a ruler on the chart **above** the row being worked to help keep your place.

BODY

With Color A, ch 126.

Row 1 (Right side)**:** Sc in second ch from hook and in each ch across: 125 sc.

Note: Loop a short piece of yarn around any stitch to mark Row 1 as **right** side.

Row 2: Ch 1, turn; sc in each sc across changing to Color B in last sc *(**Fig. 7a, page 31**)*.

When changing colors, drop the yarn to the back of work and pick up the new color from underneath. Carry unused color along edge.

Row 3: Ch 1, turn; sc in Back Loop Only of each sc across *(**Fig. 2, page 30**)*.

Row 4 AND ALL WRONG SIDE ROWS: Ch 1, turn; sc in both loops of each st across changing colors in last sc.

Follow Chart from **right** to **left**, working from W to Y once, then from X to Z once.

KEY

- Color A (Grey) sc
- Color A (Grey) LDC
- Color B (Blue) sc
- Color B (Blue) LDC

CHART

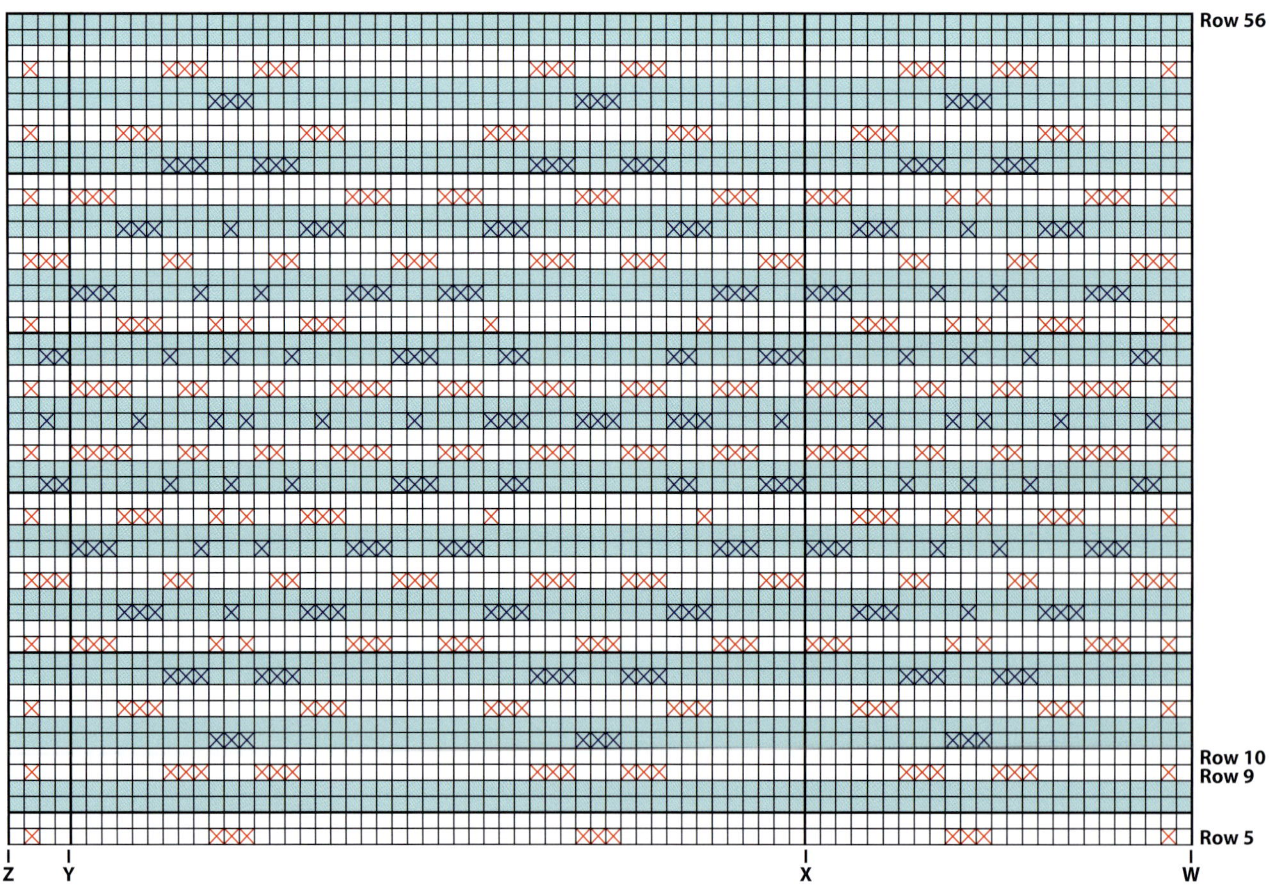

Row 5: Ch 1, turn; sc in BLO of first sc, work LDC, sc in BLO of next 11 sc, work 3 LDC, (sc in BLO of next 21 sc, work 3 LDC) 4 times, sc in BLO of next 11 sc, work LDC, sc in BLO of last sc: 17 LDC and 108 sc.

Row 7: Ch 1, turn; sc in BLO of each sc across.

Row 9: Ch 1, turn; sc in BLO of first sc, work LDC, sc in BLO of next 8 sc, work 3 LDC, sc in BLO of next 3 sc, work 3 LDC, ★ sc in BLO of next 15 sc, work 3 LDC, sc in BLO of next 3 sc, work 3 LDC; repeat from ★ 3 times **more**, sc in BLO of next 8 sc, work LDC, sc in BLO of last sc: 32 LDC and 93 sc.

Rows 10-212: Working in same manner, follow Chart Rows 10-56 once; then follow Rows 5-56, 3 times.

Rows 213 and 214: Repeat Rows 5 and 6; do **not** finish off.

EDGING

Rnd 1: Ch 1, turn; working in both loops, 3 sc in first sc, sc in each sc across to last sc, 3 sc in last sc; sc evenly across end of rows; working in free loops of beginning ch ***(Fig. 3b, page 30)***, 3 sc in first ch, sc in each ch across to last ch, 3 sc in last ch; sc evenly across end of rows working around carried strands; join with slip st to first sc.

Rnd 2: Ch 1, turn; sc in both loops of each sc around working 3 sc in each corner sc; join with slip st to first sc, finish off.

Rnd 3: With **right** side facing and working in BLO, join Color B with dc in any sc ***(see Joining With Dc, page 30)***; dc in next sc and in each sc around working 3 dc in each corner sc; join with slip st to first dc, finish off.

Rnd 4: With **right** side facing and working in BLO, join Color A with sc in any dc ***(see Joining With Sc, page 30)***; sc in each dc around working 3 sc in each corner dc; join with slip st to first sc.

Rnd 5: Ch 1, do **not** turn; working from **left** to **right**, ★ insert hook in sc to **right** of hook ***(Fig. A)***, YO and draw through, under and to left of loop on hook (2 loops on hook) ***(Fig. B)***, YO and draw through both loops on hook ***(Fig. C) (reverse sc made, Fig. D)***; repeat from ★ around; join with slip st to first st, finish off.

Design inspired by Kathleen Garen.

Fig. A

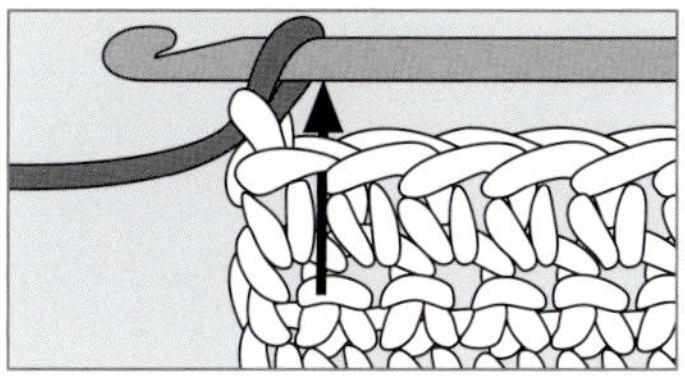

Fig. B

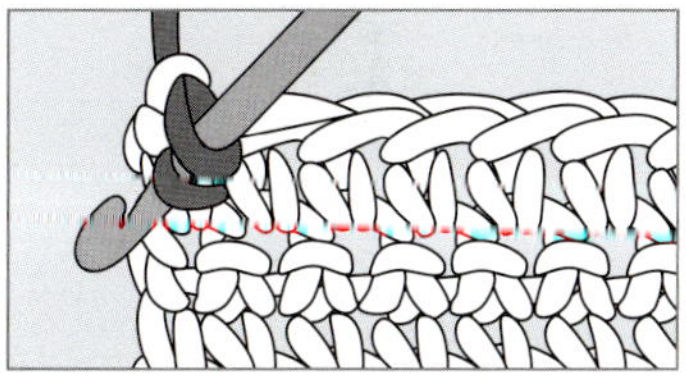

Fig. C

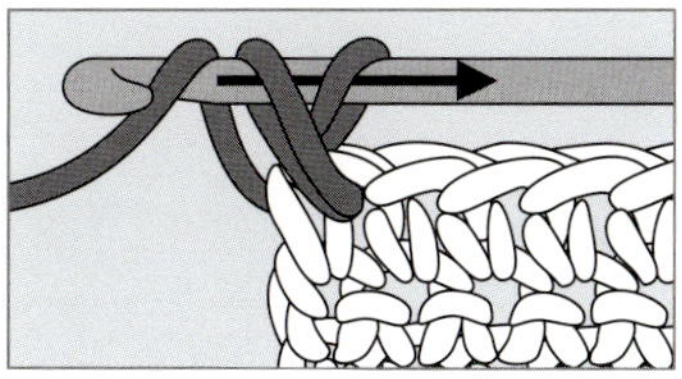

Fig. D

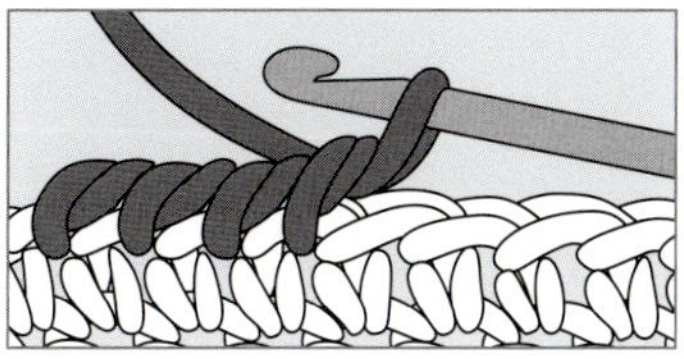

Lacy Texture

EASY

Finished Measurement: 49" x 66½" (124.5 cm x 169 cm)

SHOPPING LIST

Yarn (Medium Weight) 4

[3.5 ounces, 175 yards
(100 grams, 160 meters)
per skein]:

- ☐ Main Color (Grey) - 14 skeins
- ☐ Contrasting Color (Pink) - 3 skeins

Crochet Hook

- ☐ Size J (6 mm) **or** size needed for gauge

GAUGE INFORMATION

In pattern,
13 sc = 4" (10 cm),
6 rows = 3½" (9 cm)

Gauge Swatch: 4½" wide x 3½" high (11.5 cm x 9 cm)

With Main Color, ch 17.

Work same as Body, page 22, for 6 rows: 15 sc.

Finish off.

STITCH GUIDE

FRONT POST DOUBLE CROCHET ***(abbreviated FPdc)***

YO, insert hook from **front** to **back** around post of dc indicated ***(Fig. 6, page 31)***, YO and pull up a loop ***(Fig. A)*** (3 loops on hook), (YO and draw through 2 loops on hook) twice.

BACK POST DOUBLE CROCHET ***(abbreviated BPdc)***

YO, insert hook from **back** to **front** around post of dc indicated ***(Fig. 6, page 31)***, YO and pull up a loop (3 loops on hook) ***(Fig. B)***, (YO and draw through 2 loops on hook) twice.

POPCORN (uses next sp)

4 Dc in sp indicated, drop loop from hook, insert hook in first dc of 4-dc group, hook dropped loop and draw through st ***(Fig. C)***.

V-St

(Dc, ch 1, dc) in st or sp indicated.

PICOT

Ch 3, sc in third ch from hook.

Fig. A

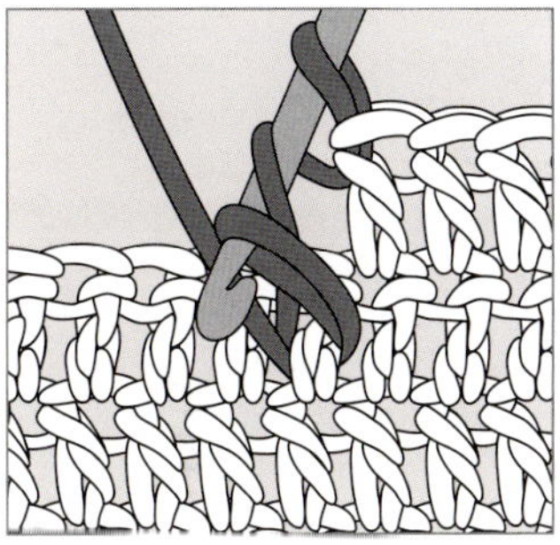

Fig. B

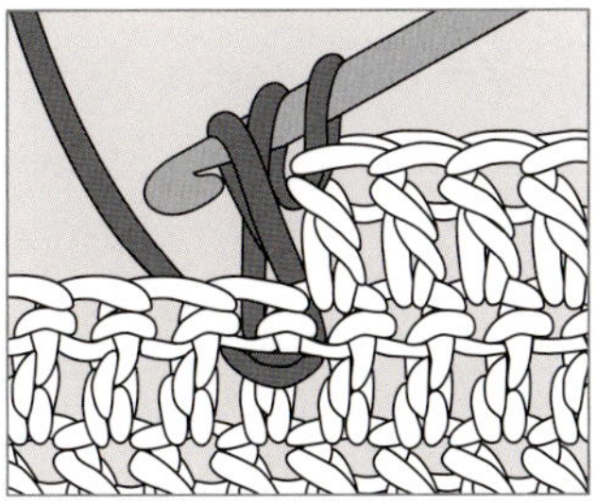

Fig. C

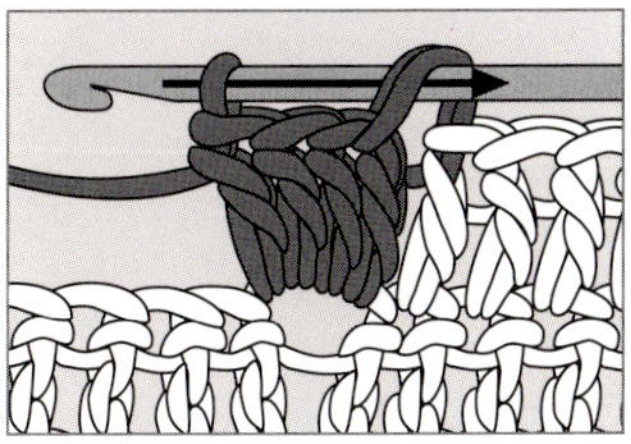

BODY

With Main Color, ch 141, place marker in third ch from hook for Edging placement.

Row 1 (Wrong side)**:** Dc in fourth ch from hook **(3 skipped chs count as first dc)** and in each ch across; finish off: 139 dc.

Note: Loop a short piece of yarn around the **back** of any stitch on Row 1 to mark **right** side.

Row 2: With **right** side facing, join Contrasting Color with dc in first dc ***(see Joining With Dc, page 30)***; work FPdc around next dc, (work BPdc around next 3 dc, work FPdc around next dc) across to last dc, dc in last dc; finish off.

Row 3: With **wrong** side facing, join Main Color with dc in first dc; skip next 2 sts, (2 dc, ch 1, 2 dc) in next st, ★ skip next 3 sts, (2 dc, ch 1, 2 dc) in next st; repeat from ★ across to last 3 sts, skip next 2 sts, dc in last dc: 34 ch-1 sps and 138 dc.

Row 4: Ch 3 **(counts as first dc, now and throughout)**, turn; ★ work (Popcorn, ch 3, Popcorn) in next ch-1 sp, ch 1; repeat from ★ across, skip next 2 dc, dc in last dc: 34 ch-3 sps and 68 Popcorns.

Row 5: Ch 2 **(counts as first hdc)**, turn; hdc in first dc, 4 hdc in each ch-3 sp across, skip next Popcorn, hdc in last dc: 139 hdc.

Row 6: Ch 1, turn; sc in Back Loop Only of each hdc across ***(Fig. 2, page 30)***.

Row 7: Ch 3, turn; dc in both loops of next sc and in each sc across; finish off.

Repeat Rows 2-7 for pattern until Body measures approximately 61" (155 cm) from beginning ch, ending by working Row 2.

Last Row: With **wrong** side facing, join Main Color with sc in first dc ***(see Joining With Sc, page 30)***; sc in each st across; do **not** finish off.

EDGING

Rnd 1: Ch 4 **(counts as first dc plus ch 1)**, turn; dc in first sc, (skip next 2 sc, work V-St in next sc) across, ch 1 (corner), work V-St in same sc as last V-St; work V-Sts evenly across end of rows; working in free loops of beginning ch ***(Fig. 3b, page 30)***, work (V-St, ch 1, V-St) in marked ch, remove marker, (skip next 2 chs, work V-St in next ch) across, ch 1, work V-St in same ch as last V-St; work V-Sts evenly across end of rows, work V-St in same sc as first dc, ch 1; join with slip st to first dc.

Rnds 2 and 3: Turn; slip st in first ch, ch 4, dc in same st, ★ work V-St in ch of each V-St across to next corner ch, (V-St, ch 1, V-St) in corner ch; repeat from ★ 2 times **more**, work V-St in ch of each V-St across and in same ch as first dc, ch 1; join with slip st to first dc.

Finish off.

Rnd 4: With **wrong** side facing, join Contrasting Color with hdc in last ch-1 sp made ***(see Joining With Hdc, page 30)***; 2 hdc in same sp, 3 hdc in each ch-1 sp around; join with slip st to first hdc, finish off.

Rnd 5: With **right** side facing, join Main Color with dc in sp **between** first and last 3-hdc group made ***(Fig. 4, page 31)***; 2 dc in same sp, 3 dc in sp **between** each 3-hdc group around; join with slip st to first dc.

Rnd 6: Ch 1, turn; sc in same st as joining, work Picot, sc in next dc, work Picot, ★ (skip next dc, sc in next 2 dc, work Picot) across to last 2 dc on same side, skip next dc, (sc in next dc, work Picot) twice; repeat from ★ 2 times **more**, (skip next dc, sc in next 2 dc, work Picot) across to last dc, skip last dc; join with slip st to first sc, finish off.

Design by Barbara Shaffer.

Shadow Box

EASY

Finished Measurement: 47" x 64"
(119.5 cm x 162.5 cm)

SHOPPING LIST

Yarn (Medium Weight) MEDIUM 4

[3.5 ounces, 205 yards
(100 grams, 187 meters) per skein]:

- ☐ Main Color (Grey) - 12 skeins
- ☐ Color A (Orange) - 3 skeins
- ☐ Color B (Yellow) - 3 skeins

Crochet Hook

- ☐ Size 7 (4.5 mm)
  or size needed for gauge

GAUGE INFORMATION

In pattern,
16 sts and 10 rows = 3¾" (9.5 cm)
Gauge Swatch: 5" wide x 3¾" high
(12.75 cm x 9.5 cm)
With Main Color, ch 22.
Work same as First Shadow Box Section for 10 rows: 21 sts.
Finish off.

STITCH GUIDE

TREBLE CROCHET ***(abbreviated tr)***
YO twice, insert hook in st indicated, YO and pull up a loop (4 loops on hook), (YO and draw through 2 loops on hook) 3 times.

Each row is worked across length of afghan.

FIRST SHADOW BOX SECTION

With Main Color, ch 274.

Row 1 (Wrong side)**:** Sc in second ch from hook and in each ch across: 273 sc.

Note: Loop a short piece of yarn around **back** of any stitch on Row 1 to mark **right** side.

Row 2: Ch 2 **(does not count as a st)**, turn; hdc in **both** loops of first sc, hdc in Back Loop Only of each sc across to last sc ***(Fig. 2, page 30)***, hdc in **both** loops of last sc.

Row 3: Ch 2, turn; hdc in **both** loops of first hdc, hdc in Back Loop Only of next hdc, working **behind** next hdc ***(Fig. 5, page 31)***, tr in free loop of sc in row **below** ***(Fig. 3a, page 30)***, ★ skip hdc in front of tr, hdc in Back Loop Only of next 3 hdc, working **behind** next hdc, tr in sc in row **below**; repeat from ★ across to last 3 hdc, skip hdc in front of tr, hdc in Back Loop Only of next hdc, hdc in **both** loops of last hdc: 68 tr and 205 hdc.

Row 4: Ch 2, turn; hdc in **both** loops of first hdc, hdc in Back Loop Only of each st across to last hdc, hdc in **both** loops of last hdc: 273 hdc.

Row 5: Ch 2, turn; hdc in **both** loops of first hdc, hdc in Back Loop Only of next hdc, working **behind** next hdc, tr in free loop of tr in row **below**, ★ skip hdc in front of tr, hdc in Back Loop Only of next 3 hdc, working **behind** next hdc, tr in free loop of tr in row **below**; repeat from ★ across to last 3 hdc, skip hdc in front of tr, hdc in Back Loop Only of next hdc, hdc in **both** loops of last hdc: 68 tr and 205 hdc.

Repeat Rows 4 and 5 for Shadow Box pattern until section measures approximately 7" (18 cm), ending by working Row 5; finish off.

STRIPE

When joining yarn and finishing off, always leave a 7" (18 cm) end to be worked into fringe.

Row 1: With **right** side facing and working in both loops, join Color A with sc in first hdc *(see Joining With Sc, page 30)*; sc in each st across; finish off.

Row 2: With **right** side facing, join Color B with sc in **both** loops of first sc; sc in Back Loop Only of each sc across to last sc, sc in **both** loops of last sc; finish off.

Row 3: With Color A, repeat Row 2.

Row 4: With **right** side facing, join Color B with sc in **both** loops of first sc; sc in Back Loop Only of next sc, working in **front** of next sc, dc in free loop of st in row **below**, ★skip sc behind dc, sc in Back Loop Only of next 3 sc, working in **front** of next sc, dc in free loop of st in row **below**; repeat from ★ across to last 3 sc, skip sc behind dc, sc in Back Loop Only of next sc, sc in **both** loops of last sc; finish off: 68 dc and 205 sc.

Row 5: With **right** side facing, join Color A with sc in **both** loops of first sc; working in **front** of next sc, dc in free loop of sc in row **below**, ★ skip sc behind dc, sc in Back Loop Only of next st, working in **front** of next sc, dc in free loop of sc in row **below**; repeat from ★ across to last 2 sc, skip sc behind dc, sc in **both** loops of last sc; finish off: 136 dc and 137 sc.

Row 6: With **right** side facing, join Color B with sc in **both** loops of first sc; sc in Back Loop Only of next dc, working in **front** of next sc, dc in free loop of dc in row **below**, ★ skip sc behind dc, sc in Back Loop Only of next 3 sts, working in **front** of next sc, dc in free loop of dc in row **below**; repeat from ★ across to last 3 sc, skip sc behind dc, sc in Back Loop Only of next sc, sc in **both** loops of last sc; finish off: 68 dc and 205 sc.

Rows 7-10: Repeat Rows 3-6.

Row 11: With Color A, repeat Row 2.

NEXT SHADOW BOX SECTION

Row 1: With **wrong** side facing, join Main Color with sc in **both** loops of first sc; sc in Front Loop Only of each sc across to last sc, sc in **both** loops of last sc; do **not** finish off.

Work same as First Shadow Box Section, beginning with Row 2.

Continue to alternate working Stripe and Shadow Box Section for a total of 5 Shadow Box Sections; do **not** finish off.

Trim - First Side: Turn; slip st in each st across; finish off.

Trim - Second Side: With **right** side facing and working in free loops of beginning ch *(Fig. 3b, page 30)*, join Main Color with slip st in first ch; slip st in each ch across; finish off.

FRINGE

Holding 2 strands of matching color together, each 14" (35.5 cm) long, add fringe evenly spaced across short edges of afghan on Shadow Box Sections *(Figs. 8a & b, page 31)*. Add one strand of matching color fringe in each row across each Stripe in same manner, pulling yarn ends of same color through loop.

Design by Kathleen Garen.

Geometric Squares

EASY +

Finished Measurement: 44" x 65½" (112 cm x 166.5 cm)

SHOPPING LIST

Yarn (Light Weight) LIGHT 3

[5 ounces, 381 yards

(141 grams, 348 meters) per skein]:

- ☐ Color A (Cream) - 6 skeins
- ☐ Color B (Pink) - 4 skeins

Crochet Hook

- ☐ Size G (4 mm)
  or size needed for gauge

GAUGE INFORMATION

In pattern,
16 sts = 3½" (9 cm),
12 rows = 2½" (6.25 cm)

Gauge Swatch: 6" wide x 2½" high (15.25 cm x 6.25 cm)

With Color A, ch 28.

Work same as Body for 12 rows: 27 sts.

Finish off.

Each row is worked across length of afghan. When joining yarn and finishing off, always leave a 7" (18 cm) end to be worked into fringe.

BODY

With Color A, ch 300.

Row 1 (Right side)**:** Sc in second ch from hook and in each ch across; finish off: 299 sc.

Note: Loop a short piece of yarn around any stitch to mark Row 1 as **right** side.

Row 2: With **wrong** side facing, join Color B with sc in first sc ***(see Joining With Sc, page 30)***; (ch 1, skip next st, sc in next 3 sts) twice, ★ (ch 1, skip next st, sc in next st) 4 times, (ch 1, skip next st, sc in next 3 sts) twice; repeat from ★ across to last 2 sts, ch 1, skip next st, sc in last sc; finish off: 111 chs and 188 sc.

Row 3: With **right** side facing, join Color A with sc in first sc; working in **front** of previous row *(Fig. 5, page 31)*, dc in skipped st in row **below** next ch, ★ † ch 1, skip next sc, sc in next sc, ch 1, skip next sc, dc in skipped st in row **below** next ch †, repeat from † to † once **more**, (sc in next sc, dc in skipped st in row **below** next ch) 4 times; repeat from ★ across to last 9 sts, then repeat from † to † twice, sc in last sc; finish off: 76 chs, 111 dc, and 112 sc.

Row 4: With **wrong** side facing, join Color B with sc in first sc; ★ † ch 1, skip next dc, working **behind** previous row, dc in skipped sc in row **below** next ch, sc in next sc, dc in skipped sc in row **below** next ch †, repeat from † to † once **more**, (ch 1, skip next dc, sc in next sc) 4 times; repeat from ★ across to last 10 sts, then repeat from † to † twice, ch 1, skip next dc, sc in last sc; finish off: 111 chs, 76 dc, and 112 sc.

Row 5: With **right** side facing, join Color A with sc in first sc; working in **front** of previous row, (dc in skipped dc in row **below** next ch, sc in next 3 sts) twice, ★ (dc in skipped dc in row **below** next ch, sc in next sc) 4 times, (dc in skipped dc in row **below** next ch, sc in next 3 sts) twice; repeat from ★ across to last 2 sts, dc in skipped dc in row **below** next ch, sc in last sc; finish off: 111 dc and 188 sc.

Rows 6-9: Repeat Rows 2-5.

Row 10: With **wrong** side facing, join Color B with sc in first sc; ★ (ch 1, skip next st, sc in next sc) 4 times, (ch 1, skip next st, sc in next 3 sts) twice; repeat from ★ across to last 10 sts, (ch 1, skip next st, sc in next sc) 5 times; finish off: 113 chs and 186 sc.

Row 11: With **right** side facing, join Color A with sc in first sc; working in **front** of previous row, dc in skipped dc in row **below** next ch, (sc in next sc, dc in skipped st in row **below** next ch) 4 times, ★ † ch 1, skip next sc, sc in next sc, ch 1, skip next sc, dc in skipped dc in row **below** next ch †, repeat from † to † once **more**, (sc in next sc, dc in skipped st in row **below** next ch) 4 times; repeat from ★ across to last sc, sc in last sc; finish off: 72 chs, 113 dc, and 114 sc.

Row 12: With **wrong** side facing, join Color B with sc in first sc; ★ (ch 1, skip next dc, sc in next sc) 4 times, † ch 1, skip next dc, working **behind** previous row, dc in skipped sc in row **below** next ch, sc in next sc, dc in skipped sc in row **below** next ch †, repeat from † to † once **more**; repeat from ★ across to last 10 sts, (ch 1, skip next dc, sc in next sc) 5 times; finish off: 113 chs, 72 dc, and 114 sc.

Row 13: With **right** side facing, join Color A with sc in first sc; working in **front** of previous row, dc in skipped dc in row **below** next ch, (sc in next sc, dc in skipped dc in row **below** next ch) 4 times, ★ (sc in next 3 sts, dc in skipped dc in row **below** next ch) twice, (sc in next sc, dc in skipped st in row **below** next ch) 4 times; repeat from ★ across to last sc, sc in last sc; finish off: 113 dc and 186 sc.

Rows 14-17: Repeat Rows 10-13.

Repeat Rows 2-17 for pattern until Body measures approximately 43¾" (111 cm) from beginning ch, ending by working Row 9.

TOP TRIM

Row 1: With **wrong** side facing, join Color A with sc in first sc; (sc in next st, ch 1, skip next st) across to last 2 sts, sc in last 2 sts; finish off.

Row 2: With **right** side facing, join Color A with slip st in first sc; ch 2, skip next sc, (slip st in next ch-1 sp, ch 2, skip next sc) across to last sc, slip st in last sc; finish off.

BOTTOM TRIM

Row 1: With **wrong** side facing and working in free loops of beginning ch *(Fig. 3b, page 30)*, join Color A with sc in ch at base of first sc; (sc in next ch, ch 1, skip next ch) across to last 2 chs, sc in last 2 chs; finish off.

Row 2: Work same as Top Trim.

FRINGE

Holding 2 strands of matching color together, each 14" (35.5 cm) long, add fringe in each row across short edges of afghan *(Figs. 8a & b, page 31)*, pulling yarn ends through loop.

Design by Anne Halliday.

General Instructions

ABBREVIATIONS

BLO	Back Loop(s) Only
BPdc	Back Post double crochet(s)
BPsc	Back Post single crochet(s)
ch(s)	chain(s)
cm	centimeters
dc	double crochet(s)
FPdc	Front Post double crochet(s)
FPsc	Front Post single crochet(s)
hdc	half double crochet(s)
LDC	Long Double Crochet(s)
mm	millimeters
Rnd(s)	Round(s)
sc	single crochet(s)
sp(s)	space(s)
st(s)	stitch(es)
tr	treble crochet(s)
YO	yarn over

SYMBOLS & TERMS

★ — work instructions following ★ as many **more** times as indicated in addition to the first time.

† to † or ♥ to ♥ — work all instructions from first † to second † or first ♥ to second ♥ **as many** times as specified.

( ) or [ ] — work enclosed instructions **as many** times as specified by the number immediately following **or** work all enclosed instructions in the stitch or space indicated **or** contains explanatory remarks.

colon (:) — the number(s) given after a colon at the end of a row or round denote(s) the number of stitches or spaces you should have on that row or round.

GAUGE

Exact gauge is essential for proper size. Before beginning your project, make the sample swatch given in the individual instructions in the yarn and hook specified. After completing the swatch, measure it, counting your stitches and rows/rounds carefully. If your swatch is larger or smaller than specified, **make another, changing hook size to get the correct gauge**. Keep trying until you find the size hook that will give you the specified gauge.

CROCHET TERMINOLOGY		
UNITED STATES		INTERNATIONAL
slip stitch (slip st)	=	single crochet (sc)
single crochet (sc)	=	double crochet (dc)
half double crochet (hdc)	=	half treble crochet (htr)
double crochet (dc)	=	treble crochet (tr)
treble crochet (tr)	=	double treble crochet (dtr)
double treble crochet (dtr)	=	triple treble crochet (ttr)
triple treble crochet (tr tr)	=	quadruple treble crochet (qtr)
skip	=	miss

Yarn Weight Symbol & Names	LACE 0	SUPER FINE 1	FINE 2	LIGHT 3	MEDIUM 4	BULKY 5	SUPER BULKY 6	JUMBO 7
Type of Yarns in Category	Fingering, size 10 crochet thread	Sock, Fingering, Baby	Sport, Baby	DK, Light Worsted	Worsted, Afghan, Aran	Chunky, Craft, Rug	Super Bulky, Roving	Jumbo, Roving
Crochet Gauge* Ranges in Single Crochet to 4" (10 cm)	32-42 sts**	21-32 sts	16-20 sts	12-17 sts	11-14 sts	8-11 sts	6-9 sts	5 sts and fewer
Advised Hook Size Range	Steel*** 6 to 8, Regular hook B-1	B-1 to E-4	E-4 to 7	7 to I-9	I-9 to K-10½	K-10½ to M/N-13	M/N-13 to Q	Q and larger

*GUIDELINES ONLY: The chart above reflects the most commonly used gauges and hook sizes for specific yarn categories.

** Lace weight yarns are usually crocheted with larger hooks to create lacy openwork patterns. Accordingly, a gauge range is difficult to determine. Always follow the gauge stated in your pattern.

*** Steel crochet hooks are sized differently from regular hooks–the higher the number, the smaller the hook, which is the reverse of regular hook sizing.

JOINING WITH SC

When instructed to join with sc, begin with a slip knot on hook. Insert hook in stitch or space indicated, YO and pull up a loop, YO and draw through both loops on hook.

JOINING WITH HDC

When instructed to join with hdc, begin with a slip knot on hook. YO, holding loop on hook, insert hook in stitch or space indicated, YO and pull up a loop (3 loops on hook), YO and draw through all 3 loops on hook.

JOINING WITH DC

When instructed to join with dc, begin with a slip knot on hook. YO, holding loop on hook, insert hook in stitch or space indicated, YO and pull up a loop (3 loops on hook), (YO and draw through 2 loops on hook) twice.

BACK RIDGE OF CHAINS

Work only in loops indicated by arrows ***(Fig. 1)***.

Fig. 1

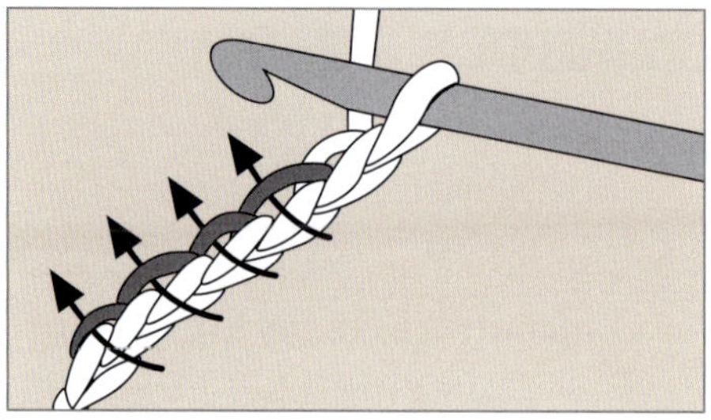

BACK & FRONT LOOPS ONLY

Work only in loop(s) indicated by arrow ***(Fig. 2)***.

Fig. 2

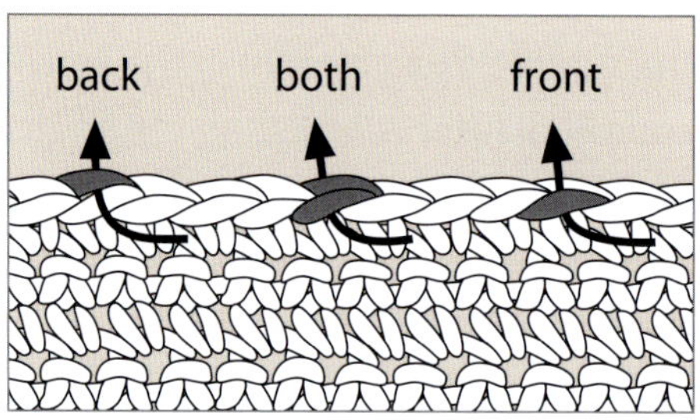

FREE LOOPS

After working in Back Loops Only on a row or round, there will be a ridge of unused loops. These are called the free loops. Later, when instructed to work in the free loops of the same row or round, work in these loops ***(Fig. 3a)***.

Fig. 3a

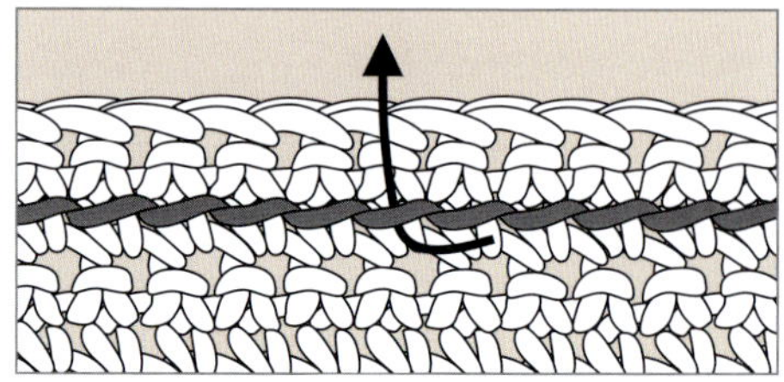

When instructed to work in free loops of a chain, work in loop indicated by arrow ***(Fig. 3b)***.

Fig. 3b

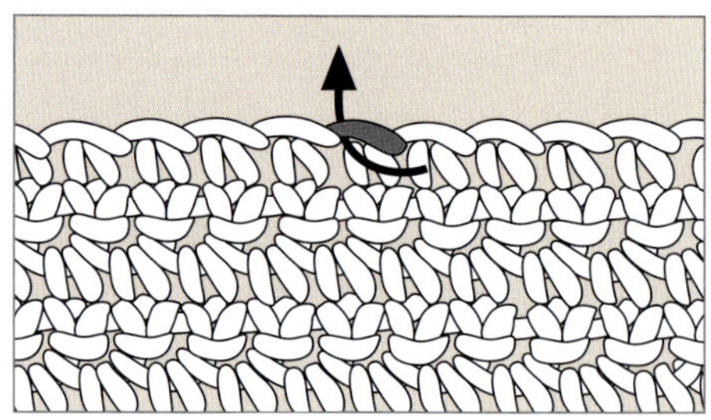

CROCHET HOOKS																	
U.S.	B-1	C-2	D-3	E-4	F-5	G-6	7	H-8	I-9	J-10	K-10½	L-11	M/N-13	N/P-15	P/Q	Q	S
Metric - mm	2.25	2.75	3.25	3.5	3.75	4	4.5	5	5.5	6	6.5	8	9	10	15	16	19

BEGINNER	Projects for first-time crocheters using basic stitches. Minimal shaping.
EASY	Projects using yarn with basic stitches, repetitive stitch patterns, simple color changes, and simple shaping and finishing.
INTERMEDIATE	Projects using a variety of techniques, such as basic lace patterns or color patterns, mid-level shaping and finishing.
EXPERIENCED	Projects with intricate stitch patterns, techniques and dimension, such as non-repeating patterns, multi-color techniques, fine threads, small hooks, detailed shaping and refined finishing.

WORKING IN SPACE BETWEEN STITCHES

When instructed to work in space **between** stitches, insert hook in space indicated by arrow ***(Fig. 4)***.

Fig. 4

WORKING IN FRONT OF, AROUND, OR BEHIND A STITCH

Work in stitch or space indicated, inserting hook in direction of arrow ***(Fig. 5)***.

Fig. 5

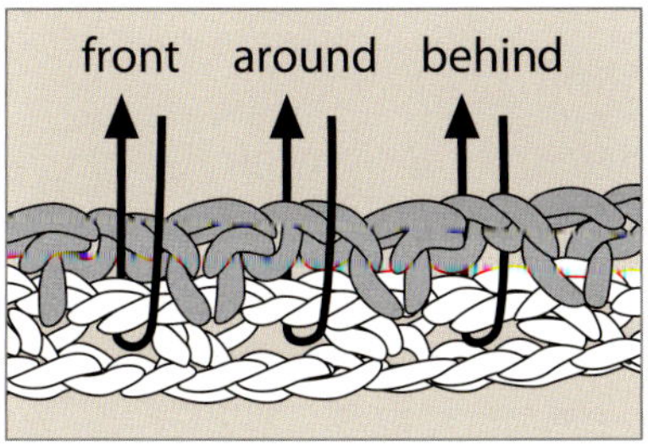

POST STITCH

Work around post of stitch indicated, inserting hook in direction of arrow ***(Fig. 6)***.

Fig. 6

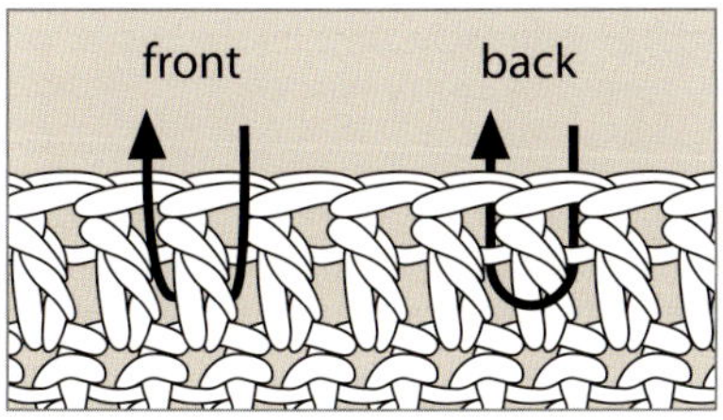

CHANGING COLORS

To change colors while working a sc, pull up a loop in stitch indicated (2 loops on hook), drop yarn, hook new yarn ***(Fig. 7a)*** and draw through both loops on hook.

Fig. 7a

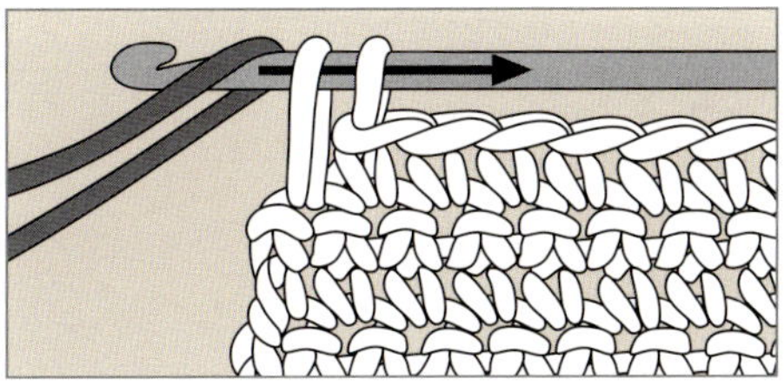

To change colors while joining with a slip st, drop yarn, insert hook in first stitch, hook new yarn and draw through st and loop on hook ***(Fig. 7b)***.

Fig. 7b

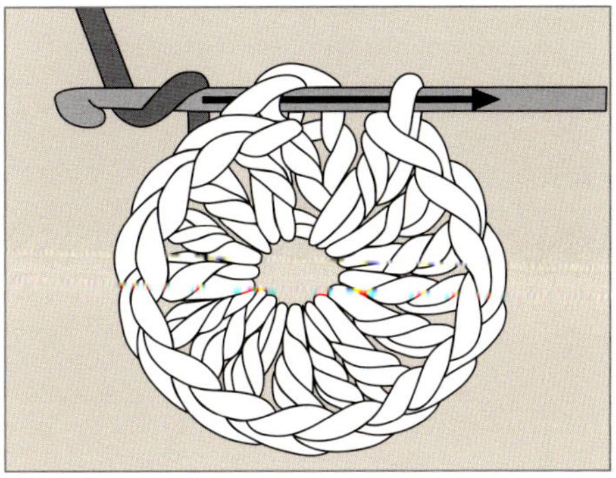

FRINGE

Cut a piece of cardboard 7" (18 cm) square. Wind the yarn loosely and evenly around the cardboard until the card is filled, then cut across one end; repeat as needed.

Hold together as many strands as specified in individual instructions; fold in half.

With **wrong** side facing and using a crochet hook, draw the folded end up through a row and pull the loose ends through the folded end ***(Fig. 8a)***; draw the knot up tightly ***(Fig. 8b)***. Repeat, spacing as specified in individual instructions.

Lay flat on a hard surface and trim the ends.

Fig. 8a

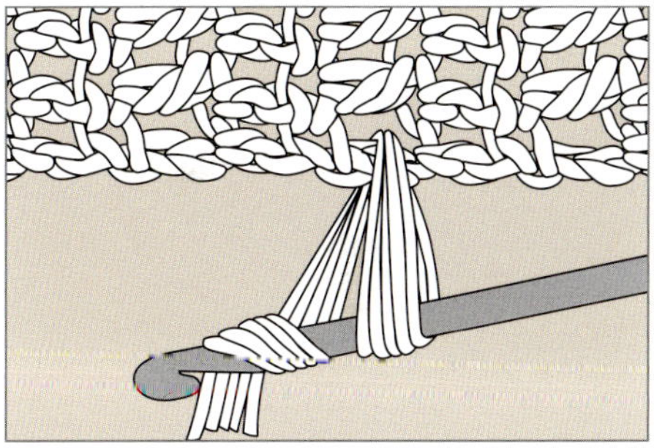

Fig. 8b

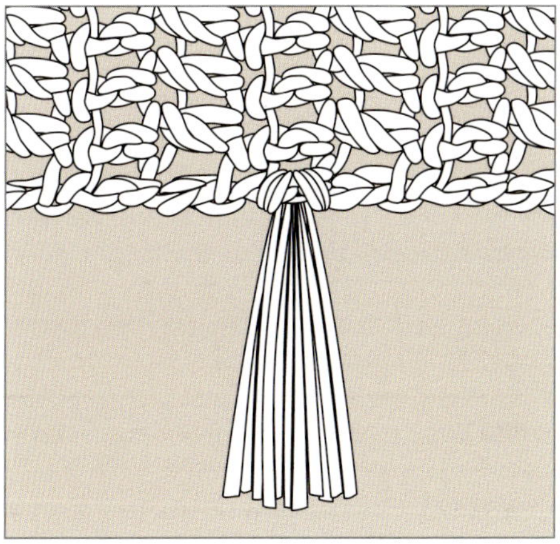

Yarn Information

The afghans in this book were made using light or medium weight yarn. Any brand of the specific weight of yarn may be used. It is best to refer to the yardage/meters when determining how many balls or skeins to purchase. Remember, to arrive at the finished size, it is the GAUGE/TENSION that is important, not the brand of yarn.

For your convenience, listed below are the yarns used to create our photography models. Because yarn manufacturers make frequent changes in their product lines, you may sometimes find it necessary to use a substitute yarn or to search for the discontinued product at alternate suppliers (locally or online).

DIAMONDS BABY BLANKET

Bernat® Softee® Baby™
Main Color - #30044 Flannel

Bernat® Softee® Baby Colors™
Color A - #51008 Purple Rainbow
Color B - #51007 Teal Rainbow

ROYAL MOSAIC

Bernat® Satin™
Color A - #04307 Sultana
Color B - #04203 Teal

SQUARE GEMS

Red Heart® Super Saver®
Tan - #334 Buff
Black - #312 Black
Green - #406 Med Thyme
Orchid - #776 Dark Orchid
Burgundy - #376 Burgundy
Maroon - #378 Claret
Brown - #336 Warm Brown
Gold - #321 Gold

GEOMETRIC DIAMONDS

Lion Brand® New Basic 175
Color A - #152 Charcoal

Bernat® Li'l Tots™
Color B - #42114 Denim

LACY TEXTURE

Lion Brand® New Basic 175
Main Color - #149 Whisper
Contrasting Color - #101 Peony

SHADOW BOX

Patons® Canadiana™
Main Color - #10012 Toasty Grey
Color A - #10628 Tangy
Color B - #10615 Cherished Yellow

GEOMETRIC SQUARES

Red Heart® Fashion Soft™
Color A - #4603 Cream
Color B - #4705 Hot Pink

We have made every effort to ensure that these instructions are accurate and complete. We cannot, however, be responsible for human error, typographical mistakes, or variations in individual work.

Afghans made and instructions tested by Janet Akins, Raymelle Greening, Kimberly Holloway, and Leticia McAllister.

Production Team: Instructional/Technical Editor - Cathy Hardy; Senior Graphic Artist - Lora Puls; Graphic Artist - Kellie McAnulty; Photo Stylist - Lori Wenger; and Photographer - Jason Masters.

Made in U.S.A.